MW00396764

The best picture:

Name

Thoughts

The best picture:

Name

_____

Thoughts

The best picture:

Name

Thoughts

The best picture:

Name

Thoughts

_____

The best picture:

Name

Thoughts

The best picture:

Name

Thoughts

The best picture:

Name

Thoughts

The best picture:

Name

_____

Thoughts

The best picture:

Name

_____

Thoughts

The best picture:

Name

Thoughts

The best picture:

Name

_____

Thoughts

_____
_____
_____
_____
_____
_____
_____
_____
_____
_____
_____

The best picture:

Name

_____

Thoughts

The best picture:

Name

Thoughts

The best picture:

Name

_____

Thoughts

_____
_____
_____
_____
_____
_____
_____
_____
_____
_____
_____
_____

The best picture:

Name

Thoughts

The best picture:

Name

Thoughts

The best picture:

Name

Thoughts

The best picture:

Name

Thoughts

The best picture:

Name

Thoughts

The best picture:

Name

Thoughts

The best picture:

Name

Thoughts

The best picture:

Name

_____

Thoughts

The best picture:

Name

Thoughts

The best picture:

Name

Thoughts

The best picture:

Name

Thoughts

The best picture:

Name

_____

Thoughts

The best picture:

Name

Thoughts

The best picture:

Name

Thoughts

The best picture:

Name

Thoughts

The best picture:

Name

Thoughts

The best picture:

Name

Thoughts

The best picture:

Name

Thoughts

The best picture:

Name

_____

Thoughts

The best picture:

Name

Thoughts

The best picture:

Name

Thoughts

The best picture:

Name

Thoughts

The best picture:

Name

Thoughts

The best picture:

Name

Thoughts

The best picture:

Name

_____

Thoughts

The best picture:

Name

Thoughts

The best picture:

Name

Thoughts

The best picture:

Name

_____

Thoughts

The best picture:

Name

_____

Thoughts

The best picture:

Name

Thoughts

The best picture:

Name

_____

Thoughts

The best picture:

Name

_____

Thoughts

The best picture:

Name

Thoughts

The best picture:

Name

Thoughts

The best picture:

Name

Thoughts

The best picture:

Name

Thoughts

The best picture:

Name

Thoughts

The best picture:

Name

_____

Thoughts

The best picture:

Name

Thoughts

The best picture:

Name

Thoughts

_____

The best picture:

Name

_____

Thoughts

The best picture:

Name

Thoughts

The best picture:

Name

Thoughts

The best picture:

Name

_____

Thoughts

The best picture:

Name

_____

Thoughts

_____
_____
_____
_____
_____
_____
_____
_____
_____
_____
_____

The best picture:

Impressum
Angaben gemäß § 5 TMG
Stefan Fanslau
Erlenweg, 4
61352 Bad Homburg
Germany

Contact:
E-Mail: stefan.fanslau@gmx.de

Made in the USA
Monee, IL
23 August 2022

12286291R00070